ELIXIR IN ACT

BUILDING SCALABLE APPLICATION WITH ELIXIR

OLIVER LUCAS JR

Preface

Elixir in Action: Building Scalable Applications with Elixir is a comprehensive guide that empowers you to harness the power of Elixir to build robust, scalable, and maintainable applications. Whether you're a seasoned developer or just starting your Elixir journey, this book will equip you with the knowledge and practical skills needed to succeed.

Elixir, with its functional programming paradigm, strong concurrency model, and rich ecosystem, offers a compelling solution for modern application development. This book delves into the core concepts of Elixir, guiding you through the process of building real-world applications.

Key Topics Covered:

Functional Programming Fundamentals: Explore the core principles of functional programming and how they are applied in Elixir.

The Elixir Ecosystem: Discover the powerful tools and libraries that make up the Elixir ecosystem, including Mix, IEx, and Ecto.

Building Concurrent Applications: Learn how to leverage Elixir's concurrency primitives to build scalable and responsive applications.

Web Development with Phoenix: Dive into the Phoenix framework and build full-stack web applications with ease.

Real-Time Applications with Phoenix LiveView: Explore the magic of LiveView and build interactive user interfaces without full page reloads.

Testing and Debugging: Master the art of writing effective tests and debugging Elixir applications.

Deployment Strategies: Learn how to deploy your Elixir applications to various platforms, including Heroku, AWS, and self-hosted environments.

This book is designed to be practical and hands-on. You'll find numerous code examples, exercises, and real-world scenarios to solidify your understanding. By the end of this book, you'll be able to confidently build and deploy scalable Elixir applications.

I hope you enjoy the journey!

Happy coding!

TABLE OF CONTENTS

Chapter 7

Chapter 8

Chapter 9

Chapter 10

Chapter 1

Introduction to Elixir

1.1 What is Elixir?

Elixir is a dynamic, functional programming language designed for building scalable and maintainable applications. It runs on the Erlang VM (BEAM), which is known for its ability to handle high concurrency and fault tolerance. This makes Elixir a powerful choice for building real-time, distributed systems.

Key features and benefits of Elixir:

Functional programming: Elixir embraces functional programming principles, which promotes writing clean, concise, and testable code.

Concurrency and fault tolerance: Built on the Erlang VM, Elixir excels at handling concurrent processes and gracefully recovering from failures.

Scalability: Elixir applications can scale horizontally, allowing you to handle increasing loads by adding more machines to your cluster.

Productivity: Elixir's strong tooling, including the Mix build tool and the IEx interactive shell, significantly boosts developer productivity.

Expressive syntax: Elixir's syntax is clean and readable, making it easy to learn and understand.

Strong community and ecosystem: Elixir has a growing and active community, with a rich ecosystem of libraries and frameworks.

Common use cases for Elixir:

Web development: Elixir's Phoenix framework is a powerful tool for building scalable and robust web applications.

Real-time applications: Elixir's ability to handle concurrency makes it ideal for building real-time systems like chat applications, game servers, and IoT devices.

Distributed systems: Elixir's distributed computing capabilities allow you to build complex, distributed systems that can scale across multiple machines.

Embedded systems: Elixir can be used to build embedded systems, such as routers and switches, that require high performance and reliability.

Overall, Elixir is a versatile and powerful language that can be used to build a wide range of applications. Its emphasis on functional programming, concurrency, and fault tolerance make it a great choice for developers who want to build reliable and scalable systems.

1.2 Why Elixir?

Why Elixir?

Elixir offers a compelling blend of features that make it an excellent choice for building robust, scalable, and maintainable applications:

1. Functional Programming Paradigm:

Immutability: Encourages writing pure functions that don't modify their input data, leading to predictable and easier-to-reason-about code.

Pattern Matching: Provides a powerful way to decompose complex data structures and write concise, expressive code.

Higher-Order Functions: Allows for elegant abstractions and functional programming techniques.

2. Concurrency and Fault Tolerance:

Built on the Erlang VM: Leverages the BEAM's proven ability to handle massive numbers of concurrent processes efficiently and reliably.

Supervisor Trees: Enables the creation of hierarchical structures of processes that monitor and restart failing processes, ensuring system resilience.

Hot Code Swapping: Allows for seamless updates to running applications without downtime.

3. Productivity and Developer Experience:

Mix Build Tool: Simplifies project management, dependency management, and task automation.

IEx Interactive Shell: Provides a powerful environment for experimenting, testing, and debugging Elixir code.

Phoenix Framework: A high-productivity framework for building web applications, offering features like channels for real-time communication and LiveView for reactive UI updates.

4. Scalability and Performance:

Distributed Systems: Elixir's ability to handle concurrency and fault tolerance makes it well-suited for building distributed systems.

High Performance: The BEAM's efficient execution model and just-in-time compilation contribute to high performance.

5. Strong Community and Ecosystem:

Active Community: A growing and supportive community of developers.

Rich Ecosystem: A variety of libraries and frameworks available to extend Elixir's capabilities.

1.3 Setting Up Your Elixir Environment

Setting Up Your Elixir Environment

Installing Elixir

1. Package Managers:

macOS:

Bash

```
brew install elixir
```
Linux:

Debian/Ubuntu:
Bash
```
sudo apt update
sudo apt install elixir
```

Fedora/CentOS:
Bash
sudo dnf install elixir

Windows:
Using Chocolatey:
Bash

choco install elixir
Manual Installation: Download the installer from the Elixir website and follow the instructions.

Verifying the Installation:

Open your terminal or command prompt.

Type `elixir -v` and press Enter.

You should see the Elixir version displayed.

Installing Elixir's Build Tool: Mix

Mix is a powerful tool for managing and compiling Elixir projects.

It's usually installed along with Elixir.

Creating Your First Elixir Project:

Open your terminal.

Navigate to your desired project directory.

Run the following command:

Bash

```
mix new hello_world
```

Navigate into the newly created directory:

Bash

```
cd hello_world
```

Running Your First Elixir Application:

Start the IEx shell:

Bash

```
iex
```

To run a simple Elixir script:
Elixir

```
iex> IO.puts "Hello, world!"
```

To compile and run your project:

Bash

```
mix run
```

Using a Text Editor or IDE:

Popular choices

Visual Studio Code with the ElixirLS extension

Vim or Neovim with Elixir plugins

Atom with the Elixir Language Server

Key features to look for:

Syntax highlighting

Code completion

Linting

Debugging

Integration with Mix

By following these steps, you'll have a solid foundation for your Elixir development journey. Remember to explore the Elixir documentation and the vibrant community for further learning and support.

Chapter 2

Functional Programming with Elixir

2.1 Elixir's Functional Core

Elixir is a functional programming language, which means it prioritizes functions as the primary building block of applications. This functional core offers several key advantages:

Immutability

Data Integrity: Once data is assigned to a variable, it cannot be changed. This prevents unintended side effects and makes code more predictable.

Concurrent Safety: Immutable data structures are inherently thread-safe, making concurrent programming easier and safer.

Pure Functions

Deterministic: A pure function always returns the same output for the same input, regardless of the program's state.

Testability: Pure functions are easier to test as they have no side effects and are isolated from external factors.

Composability: Pure functions can be combined to create more complex functions, promoting modularity and code reuse.

Pattern Matching

Expressive Power: Pattern matching allows for concise and elegant code that matches data structures against patterns.

Case Analysis: It's used to handle different data cases efficiently.

Data Extraction: Pattern matching can extract specific parts of data structures.

Higher-Order Functions

Abstraction: Higher-order functions can take functions as arguments or return functions as results, enabling powerful abstractions.

Functional Programming Paradigms: They support functional programming concepts like map, filter, reduce, and recursion.

Example: A Simple Function

```elixir
Elixir
defmodule Math do
  def add(x, y) do
    x + y
  end
end
```

In this example:

add/2 is a pure function that takes two arguments, x and y.

It returns the sum of x and y without modifying any external state.

By leveraging these functional core concepts, Elixir enables developers to write clean, concise, and maintainable code, making it an excellent choice for building robust and scalable applications.

2.2 Immutability and Pure Functions in Elixir

Immutability In Elixir, immutability is a core principle. This means that once a piece of data is created, it cannot be changed. Instead of modifying existing data, new data is created. This concept is fundamental to functional programming and has several advantages:

Predictability: Immutable data structures are easier to reason about, as their state remains consistent.

Concurrency Safety: Immutable data structures are inherently thread-safe, making concurrent programming easier.

Debugging: It's easier to debug code that doesn't have side effects.

Example of Immutability in Elixir:

```
Elixir
list = [1, 2, 3]
new_list = [4] ++ list
```

In this example, a new list `new_list` is created by concatenating `[4]` with the original `list`. The original `list` remains unchanged.

Pure Functions A pure function is a function that:

Always returns the same output for the same input.

Has no side effects.

Pure functions are essential for writing reliable and maintainable code. They make code easier to test, reason about, and refactor.

Example of a Pure Function in Elixir:

```elixir
Elixir
defmodule Math do
  def add(x, y) do
    x + y
  end
end
```

The add function is pure because:

It always returns the sum of x and y.

It doesn't modify any external state.

Why are Immutability and Pure Functions Important?

Easier to Reason About: Immutable data structures and pure functions make code more predictable and easier to understand.

Improved Concurrency: Immutable data structures are inherently thread-safe, making concurrent programming easier

Better Testability: Pure functions are easier to test, as they have no side effects and are isolated from external factors.

Enhanced Code Quality: Immutability and pure functions can lead to more reliable, maintainable, and efficient code.

By embracing immutability and pure functions, you can write more elegant, efficient, and robust Elixir code.

2.3 Pattern Matching and Recursion in Elixir

Pattern Matching

Pattern matching is a powerful technique in Elixir that allows you to match data structures against patterns. It's used extensively in function definitions, case expressions, and other constructs.

Basic Pattern Matching:

```
Elixir
defmodule MyModule do
  def greet(name) do
    IO.puts "Hello, #{name}!"
  end
end
```

In this example, the `greet/1` function takes a single argument, `name`. The pattern `name` matches any value and binds it to the variable `name`.

More Complex Patterns:

```
Elixir
defmodule MyModule do
  def factorial(0), do: 1
  def factorial(n) when n > 0, do: n * factorial(n - 1)
end
```

Here, we've defined two clauses for the `factorial/1` function:

The first clause matches when `n` is 0 and returns 1.

The second clause matches when n is greater than 0 and recursively calls itself with n - 1.

Recursion Recursion is a technique where a function calls itself directly or indirectly. It's often used in conjunction with pattern matching to solve problems that can be broken down into smaller, similar subproblems.

Example: Factorial Function

```Elixir
defmodule Math do
  def factorial(0), do: 1
  def factorial(n) when n > 0, do: n * factorial(n - 1)
end
```

The factorial function is a classic example of recursion. It breaks down the problem of calculating the factorial of n into smaller subproblems.

Key Points to Remember:

Pattern matching and recursion are powerful tools for writing concise and elegant Elixir code.

Use pattern matching to match data structures against patterns and extract specific parts.

Recursion is a technique for solving problems by breaking them down into smaller, similar subproblems.

Be careful with recursion to avoid stack overflows. Elixir's tail recursion optimization can help mitigate this.

By mastering pattern matching and recursion, you can write more expressive and efficient Elixir code.

Chapter 3

The Elixir Ecosystem

3.1 The Elixir Toolchain

The Elixir toolchain is a suite of tools that work together to provide a seamless development experience. Here are the key components:

Mix

Build Tool: Mix is the primary build tool for Elixir projects. It handles tasks like compiling code, running tests, and creating releases.

Dependency Management: Mix manages project dependencies, ensuring that your project has the necessary libraries and their correct versions.

Task Runner: Mix allows you to define custom tasks for your project, such as cleaning up the build directory or running specific tests.

IEx

Interactive Shell: IEx is an interactive shell that allows you to experiment with Elixir code, evaluate expressions, and inspect data structures.

Debugging: IEx provides powerful debugging tools, including breakpoints, step-by-step execution, and inspection of variables.

Elixir Language Server (ELS)

Code Completion: ELS provides intelligent code completion suggestions based on your project's context.

Syntax Highlighting: ELS highlights syntax errors and provides visual cues to improve code readability.

Go-to Definition: Quickly navigate to the definition of functions, modules, and macros.

Refactoring: Perform automated code refactoring tasks, such as renaming variables and functions.

Other Tools

Elixir Format: A tool for formatting Elixir code according to community-agreed-upon style guidelines.

Credo: A static analysis tool that helps identify potential issues in your code, such as unused variables, magic numbers, and performance bottlenecks.

Dialyzer: A static type checker that can help you catch errors early in the development process.

By understanding and effectively using these tools, you can significantly improve your Elixir development workflow and produce high-quality code.

3.2 Mix: The Elixir Build Tool

Mix is the primary build tool for Elixir projects. It's a versatile tool that simplifies project management, dependency management, and task automation.

Core Features of Mix:

Project Creation:

Bash

```
mix new my_project
```

This command creates a new Elixir project directory with a basic structure.

Dependency Management: Mix uses a declarative approach to manage dependencies. You specify the dependencies in a `mix.exs` file, and Mix handles fetching and compiling them.

Elixir

```
defp deps do
  [
    {:phoenix, "~> 1.7"},
    {:gettext, "~> 0.4"}
  ]
end
```

Task Runner: Mix allows you to define custom tasks for your project. For example, you can define a task to run tests, clean up the build directory, or deploy your application.

Elixir
```
defmodule MyApp.Tasks do
  use Mix.Task

  def clean do
    File.rm_rf("_build")
  end
end
```

Compilation and Execution: Mix compiles your Elixir source code into bytecode and executes it on the Erlang VM.

Bash
```
mix compile
mix run
```

Testing: Mix integrates with ExUnit, Elixir's testing framework. You can write tests and run them using Mix.

Bash

```
mix test
```

Common Mix Tasks:

`mix help`: Displays a list of available Mix tasks and their descriptions.

`mix deps.get`: Fetches dependencies specified in the `mix.exs` file.

`mix format`: Formats your code according to Elixir's style guidelines.

`mix credo`: Runs the Credo static analysis tool to check for potential issues in your code.

`mix dialyzer`: Runs the Dialyzer static type checker to identify potential type errors.

By mastering Mix, you can streamline your Elixir development workflow and build robust and scalable applications.

3.3 IEx: The Interactive Elixir Shell

IEx is a powerful interactive shell that allows you to experiment with Elixir code, evaluate expressions, and inspect data structures.[1] It's an invaluable tool for learning Elixir and debugging your applications.

Key Features of IEx:

Code Evaluation: You can directly type Elixir code into the IEx shell and execute it immediately.[2]

Elixir

```
iex> 2 + 2
4
```

Variable Inspection: IEx allows you to inspect the values of variables.

Elixir

```
iex> x = 10
10
iex> x * 2
20
```

Function Definition and Invocation: You can define functions and call them within IEx.

Elixir

```
iex> defmodule MyModule do
...>   def greet(name) do
...>     IO.puts "Hello, #{name}!"
...>   end
...> end
iex> MyModule.greet("Alice")
Hello, Alice!
```

Debugging: IEx provides debugging capabilities, including setting breakpoints and inspecting the call stack.

Elixir

```
iex> Kernel.inspect(123, depth: 2)
123
```

Connecting to a Running Application: You can connect to a running Elixir application to inspect its state and execute code.

Bash
```
iex -S mix run
```

Tips for Effective IEx Usage:

Use the h command: The h command provides help on various topics, including built-in functions, modules, and IEx commands.

Leverage the i command: The i command provides information about a specific module, function, or macro.

Take Advantage of the v command: The v command allows you to inspect the value of a variable.

Experiment and Learn: Don't be afraid to experiment with IEx. It's a great way to learn Elixir and understand how it works.

By mastering IEx, you can significantly improve your Elixir development workflow and become a more efficient developer.

Chapter 4

Building Concurrent Applications with Elixir

4.1 Processes and Actors in Elixir

Elixir, built on top of the Erlang VM, excels at handling concurrency and fault tolerance. This is largely due to its concept of processes and actors.

Processes

In Elixir, a process is a lightweight, isolated unit of execution. It has its own memory space, stack, and execution context. Processes are created using the `spawn/1` or `spawn_link/1` functions.

Key characteristics of Elixir processes:

Isolation: Processes are isolated from each other, preventing unintended side effects.

Lightweight: Creating and destroying processes is inexpensive.

Concurrency: Many processes can run concurrently on a single machine.

Fault Tolerance: If a process crashes, it doesn't affect other processes.

Actors

Actors are a higher-level abstraction built on top of processes. They communicate with each other by sending and receiving messages.

Key characteristics of Elixir actors:

Message-Based Communication: Actors communicate asynchronously by sending messages to each other.

Supervision Trees: Actors can be organized into hierarchical structures called supervision trees, which allow for graceful error handling and recovery.

State Management: Actors maintain their own state, which is updated in response to received messages.

Example of a simple actor:

```Elixir
defmodule Counter do
  defstruct [:count]

  def start_link do
    spawn_link(__MODULE__, :init, [0])
  end

  def init(count) do
    receive do
      {:increment, reply_to} ->
        reply_to.({:ok, count + 1})
        init(count + 1)
      {:decrement, reply_to} ->
        reply_to.({:ok, count - 1})
        init(count - 1)
      {:get_count, reply_to} ->
        reply_to.({:ok, count})
        init(count)
    end
  end
end
```

In this example, the `Counter` actor can receive three types of messages: `:increment`, `:decrement`, and `:get_count`. It updates its internal state accordingly and sends a reply to the sender of the message.

By understanding processes and actors, you can build highly concurrent and fault-tolerant Elixir applications.

4.2 Message Passing and Supervision Trees

Message Passing

In Elixir, processes communicate with each other by sending and receiving messages. This asynchronous communication model is fundamental to building concurrent and fault-tolerant systems.

How it works:

Sending a message: A process sends a message to another process using the `send/2` or `GenServer.cast/2`functions.

Receiving a message: A process receives messages using the `receive` construct. This construct blocks until a message arrives or a timeout occurs.

Example:

```
Elixir
defmodule Greeter do
  def start_link(name) do
    spawn_link(__MODULE__, :init, [name])
  end

  def init(name) do
```

```
  receive do
    {:greet, reply_to} ->
      reply_to.{"Hello, #{name}!"}
      init(name)
  end
 end
end
```

Supervision Trees

A supervision tree is a hierarchical structure of processes, where a parent process supervises its child processes. If a child process fails, the supervisor can take actions like restarting it, replacing it, or terminating the entire supervision tree.

Why use supervision trees:

Fault Tolerance: By organizing processes into supervision trees, you can ensure that your system can recover from failures.

Scalability: Supervision trees can be easily scaled horizontally by adding more supervisor processes.

Management: Supervision trees provide a structured way to manage and monitor your system.

Example of a simple supervision tree:

Elixir
```
defmodule MySupervisor do
 use Supervisor

 def start_link do
  Supervisor.start_link(__MODULE__, :start_link, [])
 end
```

```
def init(_) do
  children = [
    worker(MyWorker, [arg1, arg2])
  ]
  Supervisor.init(children, strategy: :one_for_one)
  end
end
```

In this example, MySupervisor supervises MyWorker. If MyWorker fails, the supervisor can restart it or terminate the entire supervision tree, depending on the specified strategy.

By understanding message passing and supervision trees, you can build robust and scalable Elixir applications that can handle failures gracefully and adapt to changing conditions.

4.3 GenServer and Task

GenServer

GenServer is a powerful behavior for building stateful servers in Elixir. It's commonly used to create long-running processes that handle requests, maintain state, and respond to queries.

Key features of GenServer:

Stateful: GenServers can maintain state, which can be updated in response to messages.

Asynchronous: GenServers handle requests asynchronously, allowing for efficient handling of concurrent requests.

Error Handling: GenServers can handle errors gracefully and can be supervised to ensure system reliability.

Example of a simple GenServer:

```elixir
Elixir
defmodule CounterServer do
  use GenServer

  def start_link(initial_value) do
    GenServer.start_link(__MODULE__, initial_value, [])
  end

  def init(initial_value) do
    {:ok, initial_value}
  end

  def handle_call(:increment, _from, state) do
    {:reply, state + 1, state + 1}
  end
end
```

Task

Tasks are lightweight processes that are used to perform background tasks. They are often used for fire-and-forget operations, such as sending notifications or performing long-running calculations.

Key features of Tasks:

Lightweight: Tasks are less resource-intensive than GenServers.

Fire-and-Forget: Tasks can be used to perform tasks without waiting for the result.

Simple: Tasks are easier to use than GenServers for simple background tasks.

Example of a simple Task:

```
Elixir
Task.start(fn ->
  # Perform some background task
  IO.puts "Task started"
  :timer.sleep(5000)
  IO.puts "Task finished"
end)
```

When to use GenServer or Task:

GenServer: Use GenServer for stateful processes that need to handle requests and maintain state over time.

Task: Use Task for simple, fire-and-forget tasks that don't require state or complex interactions.

By understanding GenServer and Task, you can build robust and scalable Elixir applications.

Chapter 5

Data Modeling with Ecto

5.1 Database Interactions with Ecto

Ecto is a powerful data mapping library for Elixir that provides a clean and efficient way to interact with databases. It abstracts away many of the complexities of database interactions, allowing you to focus on your application logic.

Core Concepts of Ecto

1. Schema

Defines the structure of your database tables.

Specifies the fields, types, and constraints for each table.

Example:

```
Elixir
defmodule MyApp.Repo.PostsSchema do
  use Ecto.Schema

  schema "posts" do
    field :title, :string
    field :body, :string
    field :published_at, :naive_datetime

    timestamps()
  end
end
```

2. Changeset

Represents a change to a schema.

Used to validate, cast, and transform data before inserting or updating it in the database.

Example:

Elixir
```
changeset = %MyApp.Post{}
|> PostSchema.changeset(%{title: "New Post", body: "Post content"})
```

3. Repository

Provides a layer of abstraction over database operations.

Defines functions for creating, reading, updating, and deleting records.

Example:

Elixir
```
defmodule MyApp.Repo.PostsRepo do
  use Ecto.Repo

  alias MyApp.Repo.Posts

  def get_post!(id), do: Repo.get!(Posts, id)

  def list_posts do
    Repo.all(Posts)
  end
end
```

Common Database Operations with Ecto

Creating Records:

```elixir
Elixir
changeset = %Post{}
|> PostSchema.changeset(%{title: "New Post", body: "Post content"})

Repo.insert!(changeset)
```

Reading Records:

```elixir
Elixir
post = Repo.get!(Posts, 123)
```

Updating Records:

```elixir
Elixir
post = Repo.get!(Posts, 123)
changeset = PostSchema.changeset(post, %{title: "Updated Title"})
Repo.update!(changeset)
```

Deleting Records:

```elixir
Elixir
post = Repo.get!(Posts, 123)
Repo.delete!(post)
```

Ecto's Advantages

Strong Type System: Helps prevent runtime errors and improves code reliability.

Query Builder: Provides a flexible query builder for complex queries.

Migrations: Simplifies database schema changes.

Associations: Handles relationships between different models.

Transactions: Ensures data consistency across multiple operations.

By leveraging Ecto's powerful features, you can efficiently and effectively interact with your database in Elixir applications.

5.2 Schemas and Migrations in Ecto

Schemas

In Ecto, a schema defines the structure of a database table. It specifies the fields, their data types, and any constraints or validations that should be applied to the data.

Example:

Elixir
```
defmodule MyApp.Repo.PostsSchema do
  use Ecto.Schema

  schema "posts" do
    field :title, :string
    field :body, :string
    field :published_at, :naive_datetime

    timestamps()
  end
end
```

In this example:

`title` and `body` are string fields.

`published_at` is a naive datetime field.

`timestamps()` adds `inserted_at` and `updated_at` fields for tracking when records are created and modified.

Migrations

Migrations are used to modify the database schema over time. They allow you to add, remove, or modify tables and columns in a controlled and versioned manner.

Example:

Elixir

```
defmodule MyApp.Repo.Migrations.CreatePosts do
  use Ecto.Migration

  def change do
    create table(:posts) do
      add :title, :string
      add :body, :string
      add :published_at, :naive_datetime

      timestamps()
    end
  end
end
```

Running Migrations: To run a migration, use the `mix ecto.migrate` command. This will execute all pending migrations.

Reversing Migrations: To undo a migration, use the `mix ecto.rollback` command. This will revert the last migration.

Key Points to Remember:

Schema Validation: Ecto automatically validates data based on the defined schema.

Data Casting: Ecto automatically casts data to the correct data type.

Associations: Ecto supports various types of associations, including one-to-one, one-to-many, and many-to-many.

Migrations: Use migrations to safely evolve your database schema over time.

Ecto Repo: The `Ecto.Repo` module provides functions for interacting with the database, such as inserting, updating, and deleting records.

By understanding schemas and migrations, you can effectively design and evolve your database schema in Elixir.

5.3 Queries and Changesets in Ecto

Queries

Ecto provides a powerful query builder that allows you to construct complex queries using a fluent interface.

Basic Queries:

```
Elixir
# Get all posts
posts = Repo.all(Post)
```

```
# Get a specific post
post = Repo.get!(Post, 123)
```

Filtering and Sorting:

```
Elixir
# Get all published posts
published_posts = Repo.all(Post, where: p -> p.published_at != nil)

# Get the latest 5 posts
latest_posts = Repo.all(Post, order_by: [desc: :published_at], limit:
5)
```

Joins:

```
Elixir
# Get posts with their author
query = from p in Post,
  join: a in Author,
  on: p.author_id == a.id,
  select: %{post: p, author: a}

Repo.all(query)
```

Changesets

Changesets are used to validate, cast, and transform data before inserting or updating it in the database. They provide a convenient way to handle data integrity and security.

Creating a Changeset:

```elixir
Elixir
changeset = %Post{}
|> PostSchema.changeset(%{title: "New Post", body: "Post content"})
```

Validating Changesets:

```elixir
Elixir
if changeset.valid? do
  Repo.insert!(changeset)
else
  IO.inspect changeset.errors
end
```

Customizing Changesets:

```elixir
Elixir
defmodule MyApp.Post do
  use Ecto.Schema

  schema "posts" do
    field :title, :string
    field :body, :string

    timestamps()
  end

  @required_fields [:title, :body]

  def changeset(post, params \\ %{}) do
    post
    |> cast(params, @required_fields)
```

```
    |> validate_required(@required_fields)
  end
end
```

By understanding queries and changesets, you can effectively interact with your database and ensure data integrity in your Elixir applications.

Chapter 6

Building Web Applications with Phoenix

6.1 The Phoenix Framework

Phoenix is a powerful and productive framework for building web applications with Elixir. It leverages the Erlang VM's concurrency model to handle high traffic and provides a robust set of features for building modern web applications.

Key Features of Phoenix:

Model-View-Controller (MVC) Architecture: Phoenix follows the MVC pattern, providing a clear separation of concerns.

Plug-Based Pipeline: Phoenix uses a pipeline of plugs to handle incoming requests and generate responses.

Channel System: Enables real-time, bidirectional communication between the client and server.

LiveView: A powerful framework for building interactive web interfaces without full page reloads.

Strong Community and Ecosystem: Phoenix has a large and active community, with many libraries and tools available.

Basic Structure of a Phoenix Application:

Router: Defines the routes for your application, mapping URLs to controllers and actions.

Controller: Handles incoming requests, processes data, and renders templates or redirects to other controllers.

View: Renders HTML templates, often using templates like EEx or HTML.EEx.

Model: Represents the data layer, interacting with the database via Ecto.

Context: Encapsulates data and behavior related to a specific operation.

Channel: Handles real-time communication between the client and server.

Example of a simple Phoenix Controller:

Elixir
```
defmodule MyApp.HomeController do
  use MyApp.Web, :controller

  def index(conn, _params) do
    render(conn, "index.html")
  end
end
```

Benefits of Using Phoenix:

Scalability: Built on the Erlang VM, Phoenix can handle high concurrency and load.

Reliability: Phoenix's fault-tolerant architecture ensures that your application can recover from failures.

Productivity: The strong tooling and conventions of Phoenix can significantly increase development speed.

Real-Time Capabilities: Phoenix's Channel system allows you to build real-time features like chat, notifications, and collaborative editing.

Security: Phoenix provides built-in security features, such as protection against common web vulnerabilities.

By leveraging Phoenix's powerful features and the benefits of the Elixir language, you can build robust, scalable, and maintainable web applications.

6.2 Routing and Controllers in Phoenix

Routing

Phoenix uses a router to define the routes for your application. A route maps a URL pattern to a controller and action.

Basic Routing:

```elixir
Elixir
defmodule MyApp.Router do
  use Phoenix.Router

  pipeline :browser do
    plug :accepts, ["html"]
    plug :fetch_session
    plug :fetch_flash
    plug :protect_from_forgery
    plug :put_secure_browser_headers
  end

  pipeline :api do
    plug :accepts, ["json"]
  end
```

```
scope "/", MyApp do
  pipe_through :browser

  get "/", PageController, :index
end

scope "/api", MyApp do
  pipe_through :api

  get "/users", UserController, :index
end
end
```

In this example:

/ maps to the PageController's index action.

/api/users maps to the UserController's index action.

Controllers

Controllers handle incoming requests, process data, and render responses.

Basic Controller:

Elixir
```
defmodule MyApp.PageController do
  use MyApp.Web, :controller

  def index(conn, _params) do
    render(conn, "index.html")
  end
end
```

In this example:

The `index` action renders the `index.html` template.

Handling Parameters:

```elixir
Elixir
defmodule MyApp.PostController do
  use MyApp.Web, :controller

  def show(conn, %{"id" => id}) do
    post = Repo.get!(Post, id)
    render(conn, "show.html", post: post)
  end
end
```

Redirects and Flash Messages:

```elixir
Elixir
defmodule MyApp.UserController do
  use MyApp.Web, :controller

  def create(conn, %{"user" => user_params}) do
    changeset = User.changeset(%User{}, user_params)

    if changeset.valid? do
      User.create(changeset)
      conn
      |> put_flash(:info, "User created successfully.")
      |> redirect(to: "/")
    else
      render(conn, "new.html", changeset: changeset)
    end
  end
end
```

Key Points:

Routes: Define the URLs that your application can handle.

Controllers: Handle incoming requests and generate responses.

Plugs: Modularize common functionality like authentication, authorization, and error handling.

Contexts: Encapsulate business logic and data access.

Templates: Render HTML output using templates like EEx.

By understanding routing and controllers, you can build well-structured and scalable Phoenix applications.

6.3 Views and Templates in Phoenix

Views In Phoenix, views are responsible for rendering HTML templates. They typically handle logic related to formatting data and generating HTML.

Templates Templates are used to define the structure and content of HTML pages. Phoenix primarily uses EEx templates, which are similar to ERB templates in Ruby on Rails.

Basic Template Structure:

```
HTML
<!DOCTYPE html>
<html>
  <head>
    <title><%= @page_title %></title>
  </head>
  <body>
```

```html
    <h1><%= @heading %></h1>
    <p><%= @content %></p>
  </body>
</html>
```

Rendering Templates from Controllers:

Elixir
```elixir
defmodule MyApp.PageController do
  use MyApp.Web, :controller

  def index(conn, _params) do
      render(conn, "index.html", page_title: "Welcome", heading: "Hello, World!")
  end
end
```

Key Features of Phoenix Views and Templates:

Layout Templates: Define common layout elements like the header, footer, and navigation bar.

Helper Functions: Create reusable functions to simplify template logic.

LiveView: Build dynamic, interactive user interfaces without full page reloads.

Pipeline: Process templates through a pipeline of functions to apply transformations.

Example of a Helper Function:

Elixir
```elixir
defmodule MyApp.Web.Helpers.FormHelper do
```

```
def form(conn, form_changeset) do
  # ... form rendering logic ...
  end
end
```

Key Considerations for Effective View and Template Design:

Keep Templates Clean and Concise: Avoid complex logic in templates.

Use Helper Functions: Encapsulate common template logic in helper functions.

Leverage Layout Templates: Reduce code duplication and improve maintainability.

Consider LiveView for Interactive Features: LiveView can significantly enhance the user experience.

By understanding views and templates, you can create well-structured, maintainable, and visually appealing Phoenix applications.

Chapter 7

Real-Time Applications with Phoenix LiveView

7.1 Phoenix LiveView: A Revolutionary Approach to Web Development

Phoenix LiveView is a powerful framework built on top of Phoenix that allows you to build real-time, interactive web applications without writing JavaScript. It leverages websockets to establish a persistent connection between the client and server, enabling seamless updates to the DOM without full page reloads.

Key Features of Phoenix LiveView:

Real-time Updates: Update parts of the DOM in real-time without full page reloads.

Server-Side Rendering (SSR): Ensures SEO-friendliness and fast initial page load times.

State Management: Manages state on the server, simplifying client-side state management.

Phoenix Framework Integration: Leverages Phoenix's strengths, such as routing, controllers, and templates.

Hotwire-Inspired: Shares similarities with Hotwire, a Ruby on Rails framework, but with Elixir's unique approach.

How LiveView Works:

Client-Server Connection: A WebSocket connection is established between the client and server.

DOM Diffing: When the server-side state changes, a minimal DOM diff is calculated.

Patching the DOM: The client receives the diff and applies it to the DOM, updating only the necessary parts.

User Interactions: User interactions on the client are sent back to the server via the WebSocket connection.

Server-Side Processing: The server processes the user input, updates its state, and sends a new DOM diff to the client.

Benefits of Using LiveView:

Reduced JavaScript Complexity: Less JavaScript is required, making development simpler and faster.

Improved Performance: Real-time updates and server-side rendering lead to a better user experience.

Enhanced Security: By keeping state on the server, you can mitigate certain security risks.

Easier to Learn and Maintain: Leveraging Elixir's functional programming paradigm and Phoenix's conventions.

Common Use Cases for LiveView:

Real-time Chat Applications: Build real-time chat rooms and messaging systems.

Collaborative Editing: Enable multiple users to edit documents simultaneously.

Interactive Forms: Create dynamic forms with instant feedback and validation.

Dashboard Applications: Build data-rich dashboards with real-time updates.

Game Development: Develop browser-based games with real-time interactions.

By understanding the core concepts of Phoenix LiveView, you can build modern, interactive web applications with less effort and complexity.

7.2 Building Interactive User Interfaces with Phoenix LiveView

Phoenix LiveView provides a powerful and efficient way to build interactive user interfaces without relying heavily on JavaScript. By leveraging websockets, LiveView can update parts of the DOM in real-time, creating a seamless user experience.

Core Concepts

LiveComponent: The building block of LiveView applications. It encapsulates state, rendering logic, and event handling.

Phoenix.HTML: Used to generate HTML templates.

Phx-Change: A directive that triggers a server-side event when a DOM element changes.

LiveSocket: Manages the WebSocket connection between the client and server.

Basic LiveComponent Structure

Elixir

```
defmodule MyAppWeb.Live.CounterComponent do
  use MyAppWeb, :live_component
```

```elixir
def render(assigns) do
  ~H"""
  <div>
   <h1>Counter</h1>
   <p><%= @count %></p>
   <button phx-click="increment">Increment</button>
  </div>
  """
end

def handle_event("increment", _params, %{count: count}) do
  {:reply, {:ok, count: count + 1}}
end
end
```

Breakdown:

Component Definition: The `use MyAppWeb, :live_component` macro provides the necessary functionality for LiveComponents.

Rendering: The `render` function defines the HTML structure of the component.

Event Handling: The `handle_event` function handles user interactions. In this case, it increments the `count` state and re-renders the component.

Advanced Features

Form Handling: LiveView provides built-in support for handling form submissions and validation.

LivePatch: Allows you to update parts of the DOM without a full page reload.

LiveSocket: Enables real-time communication between clients and servers, powering features like chat, notifications, and collaborative editing.

Phx-Submit: A directive that submits a form without a full page reload.

Phx-Change: A directive that triggers a server-side event when an input element changes.

By leveraging these features, you can create dynamic and interactive user interfaces that feel native.

7.3 Real-Time Updates and State Management in Phoenix LiveView

Phoenix LiveView excels at building real-time, interactive web applications. It achieves this by effectively managing state on the server and pushing updates to the client in real-time.

State Management in LiveView

LiveView components maintain state on the server. This state is updated in response to user interactions or other events. When the state changes, the component re-renders, and the updated DOM is sent to the client.

Key Points:

Server-Side State: State is managed on the server, ensuring consistency and reliability.

State Updates: State updates are triggered by user interactions or time-based events.

Re-rendering: When the state changes, the component re-renders, and only the necessary parts of the DOM are updated.

Example:

Elixir
```
defmodule MyAppWeb.Live.CounterComponent do
 use MyAppWeb, :live_component

 def render(assigns) do
  ~H"""
   <div>
    <h1>Counter</h1>
    <p><%= @count %></p>
    <button phx-click="increment">Increment</button>
   </div>
  """
 end

 def handle_event("increment", _params, %{count: count}) do
  {:reply, {:ok, count: count + 1}}
 end
end
```

Real-Time Updates

LiveView leverages websockets to establish a persistent connection between the client and server. This connection enables real-time updates to the DOM without full page reloads.

Key Mechanisms:

DOM Diffing: When the server-side state changes, a minimal DOM diff is calculated.

Patching the DOM: The client receives the diff and applies it to the DOM, updating only the necessary parts.

Phx-Change: This directive triggers a server-side event when an input element changes, allowing for real-time validation and updates.

Example:

HTML
<input phx-change="update_input" value={@input_value}>

Whenever the user types in the input field, a `update_input` event is sent to the server. The server can then process the input and update the component's state, triggering a re-render.

By understanding these concepts, you can build highly interactive and responsive web applications with Phoenix LiveView.

Chapter 8

Testing and Debugging Elixir Applications

8.1 Unit Testing with ExUnit

ExUnit is a powerful testing framework built into Elixir. It provides a simple and elegant way to write and run tests for your Elixir applications.

Basic Test Structure:

```elixir
Elixir
defmodule MyApp.MathTest do
  use ExUnit.Case

  test "adds two numbers" do
    assert Math.add(2, 3) == 5
  end
end
```

Key Concepts:

Test Case: A module that contains one or more tests.

Test: A function that asserts a specific condition.

Assert Macros: ExUnit provides various assert macros, such as assert, refute, and assert_raise, to make assertions.

Test Fixtures: Functions that set up the test environment, such as creating test data.

Example with Test Fixture:

```elixir
Elixir
defmodule MyApp.PostTest do
  use ExUnit.Case

  setup do
    {:ok, post: %Post{title: "Test Post", body: "Test Body"}}
  end

  test "creates a post", %{post: post} do
    assert Repo.insert!(post)
  end
end
```

Running Tests: To run tests, use the `mix test` command in your terminal.

Advanced Testing Techniques:

Mock and Stub: Use `Mock` and `Stub` modules to simulate external dependencies and isolate test cases.

Test Helpers: Create helper modules to encapsulate common test setup and teardown logic.

Parameterized Tests: Use `ExUnit.ParameterizedTest` to test multiple input/output combinations.

Code Coverage: Analyze code coverage to identify areas that need more testing.

Best Practices:

Write Clear and Concise Tests: Use descriptive test names and assertions.

Isolate Tests: Avoid side effects and dependencies between tests.

Test Edge Cases: Consider boundary conditions and error scenarios.

Use Test Fixtures Effectively: Set up and tear down test data efficiently.

Automate Testing: Integrate testing into your development workflow.

By following these guidelines and leveraging ExUnit's features, you can write effective tests that ensure the quality of your Elixir applications.

8.2 Integration Testing with Plug.Test

Plug.Test is a powerful tool for testing web applications built with the Plug framework, which is the foundation of Phoenix. It allows you to simulate HTTP requests and inspect the resulting responses.

Basic Usage:

```elixir
Elixir
defmodule MyApp.EndpointTest do
  use ExUnit.Case, async: true

  test "GET / returns 200 OK" do
    conn = Plug.Test.init_conn(MyAppWeb.Endpoint)
    conn = Plug.Test.get(conn, "/")

    assert conn.status == 200
  end
end
```

Key Features of Plug.Test:

Simulating HTTP Requests: You can simulate various HTTP methods (GET, POST, PUT, DELETE, etc.) with different headers and body parameters.

Inspecting Responses: You can inspect the response status code, headers, and body.

Testing Redirects: You can test redirect responses and follow redirects.

Testing Sessions and Flash Messages: You can set and retrieve session data and flash messages.

Advanced Usage:

Elixir
```
defmodule MyApp.PostControllerTest do
  use ExUnit.Case, async: true

  test "creates a new post" do
    conn = Plug.Test.init_conn(MyAppWeb.Endpoint)
    conn = Plug.Test.post(conn, "/posts", post_params)

    assert conn.status == 302
    assert conn.redirect == "/"
    assert get_flash(conn, :info) == "Post created successfully."
  end
end
```

Best Practices for Integration Testing:

Test Different Scenarios: Cover various input values, edge cases, and error conditions.

Isolate Tests: Avoid dependencies between tests to ensure reliability.

Use Test Fixtures: Set up and tear down test data efficiently.

Focus on End-to-End Behavior: Test how different parts of your application interact.

Automate Testing: Integrate integration tests into your CI/CD pipeline.

By effectively using Plug.Test, you can ensure the quality and reliability of your Phoenix applications.

8.3 Debugging Elixir Applications

Debugging Elixir applications can be a straightforward process with the right tools and techniques. Here are some effective methods:

Using IEx

Interactive Shell: IEx provides a powerful interactive shell to inspect variables, evaluate expressions, and step through code.

Breakpoints: Set breakpoints to pause execution at specific points in your code.

Inspecting Processes: Use `Process.info/1` to get information about running processes.

Using Logger

Logging: Use the `Logger` module to log messages to the console or a file.

Log Levels: Control the verbosity of logs with different levels (debug, info, warn, error, fatal).

Custom Log Formats: Customize log formats to include timestamps, process IDs, and other relevant information.

Using Dialyzer

Static Type Checking: Dialyzer analyzes your code to identify potential type errors.

Early Error Detection: By catching type errors early, you can prevent runtime errors.

Code Quality Improvement: Dialyzer can help you write more robust and maintainable code.

Using Credo

Code Analysis: Credo checks your code for potential issues, such as unused variables, magic numbers, and style violations.

Code Quality Improvement: By following Credo's recommendations, you can improve the quality of your code.

Debugging Tools in IDEs

Visual Studio Code: Use the ElixirLS extension for debugging features like breakpoints, step-by-step execution, and variable inspection.

Vim and Neovim: Use plugins like `elixir-ls` to provide similar debugging capabilities.

Tips for Effective Debugging:

Break Down Complex Problems: Divide complex problems into smaller, more manageable parts.

Use Descriptive Variable Names: Clear variable names can make your code easier to understand and debug.

Write Clean and Readable Code: Well-structured code is easier to debug.

Leverage the Community: Seek help from the Elixir community on forums or chat channels.

Use the `iex -S mix test` Command: This command allows you to debug failing tests interactively.

By combining these techniques and tools, you can efficiently debug Elixir applications and identify and fix issues quickly. Remember to approach debugging systematically and use a combination of methods to isolate the root cause of problems.

Chapter 9

Deploying Elixir Applications

9.1 Deployment Strategies for Elixir Applications

Elixir, with its strong focus on fault-tolerance and scalability, offers various deployment strategies to ensure your applications are reliable and performant. Here are some common approaches:

1. Heroku

Pros: Easy to set up, automatic scaling, and built-in CI/CD.

Cons: Potential vendor lock-in, limited customization options, and cost considerations for larger applications.

2. AWS

Pros: Highly customizable, scalable, and offers a wide range of services.

Cons: Requires more technical expertise and configuration.

Common Services:

EC2: Virtual machines for running Elixir applications.

ECS: Container orchestration for managing and scaling Elixir applications.

EBS: Block storage for persistent data.

ELB: Load balancing to distribute traffic across multiple instances.

RDS: Relational database service for storing application data.

3. DigitalOcean

Pros: User-friendly, affordable, and provides a simple way to deploy Elixir applications.

Cons: Less flexibility and customization compared to AWS.

4. Kubernetes

Pros: Highly scalable, flexible, and provides advanced features like rolling updates and canary deployments.

Cons: Requires significant technical expertise and configuration.

5. Self-Hosted

Pros: Full control over the deployment environment, cost-effective for large-scale applications.

Cons: Requires significant infrastructure management and maintenance.

Deployment Strategies:

Rolling Deployments: Gradually roll out new versions of your application to minimize downtime.

Blue-Green Deployments: Deploy a new version alongside the old one and switch traffic once it's stable.

Canary Deployments: Roll out a new version to a small subset of users to test it before deploying to the entire user base.

Zero-Downtime Deployments: Use techniques like load balancers and process supervisors to ensure minimal downtime during deployments.

Best Practices:

Automate Deployments: Use tools like `mix release` and CI/CD pipelines to automate the deployment process.

Monitor Your Application: Use tools like `Elixir's Observer` and third-party monitoring solutions to track performance and identify issues.

Implement Rollback Strategies: Have a plan to roll back to a previous version if a new deployment fails.

Secure Your Applications: Use strong passwords, encryption, and other security measures to protect your application and user data.

Test Thoroughly: Test your application in different environments to ensure it works as expected.

By carefully considering these deployment strategies and best practices, you can deploy reliable and scalable Elixir applications.

9.2 Deploying Elixir Applications to Heroku

Heroku is a popular platform as a service (PaaS) that simplifies the deployment and management of web applications. Here's a basic guide to deploying an Elixir application to Heroku:

1. Create a Heroku Account:

Sign up for a free Heroku account.

2. Create a Heroku App:

Use the Heroku CLI or the Heroku dashboard to create a new app.

3. Configure Your Elixir Project for Heroku:

Add a `Procfile` to your project's root directory. This file specifies the commands to run your application:

web: mix phx.server

Create a `config/prod.exs` file to configure your application for production. This file should contain production-specific settings, such as database credentials and API keys.

4. Deploy to Heroku:

Using the Heroku CLI:

Bash

git push heroku main

Using the Heroku Dashboard: Deploy your app directly from the dashboard.

5. Configure Your App on Heroku:

Add Buildpacks: Heroku uses buildpacks to compile and deploy your application. You'll need to add the Elixir and Node.js buildpacks.

Configure Add-ons: Add necessary add-ons like Heroku Postgres for your database.

Set Configuration Variables: Set environment variables for your application, such as database credentials and API keys.

Additional Tips:

Use `mix release`**:** This tool helps you create releases of your Elixir application, which can be deployed to Heroku.

Leverage Heroku's CI/CD Pipelines: Automate your deployment process using Heroku CI/CD pipelines.

Monitor Your App: Use Heroku's built-in monitoring tools to track performance and identify issues.

Optimize for Performance: Use techniques like caching, code optimization, and database tuning to improve performance.

Secure Your App: Implement security best practices, such as using strong passwords, protecting API keys, and regularly updating dependencies.

By following these steps and best practices, you can successfully deploy your Elixir applications to Heroku and enjoy the benefits of a scalable and reliable platform.

9.3 Deploying Elixir Applications to AWS

AWS offers a wide range of services that can be used to deploy Elixir applications. Here are some common approaches:

1. EC2 Instances

Pros: Full control over the environment, suitable for complex setups.

Cons: Requires more manual configuration and management.

Steps:

Create EC2 Instances: Launch EC2 instances with the appropriate configuration (e.g., instance type, security groups, key pairs).

Install Elixir and Dependencies: Install Elixir and other required dependencies on the instances.

Deploy Your Application: Use `mix deploy` or other deployment tools to deploy your application to the instances.

Configure Security Groups: Allow incoming traffic to your application on the appropriate ports (e.g., HTTP, HTTPS).

2. AWS Elastic Beanstalk

Pros: Easy to set up and manage, automatic scaling.

Cons: Less flexibility and control compared to EC2.

Steps:

Create an Elastic Beanstalk Environment: Choose the platform version (e.g., 64bit Amazon Linux 2) and application type (e.g., Web Server).

Configure Environment Settings: Set environment variables and other configuration settings.

Deploy Your Application: Deploy your application using the Elastic Beanstalk console or the AWS CLI.

3. AWS Elastic Container Service (ECS)

Pros: Highly scalable, efficient, and allows for container orchestration.

Cons: Requires more technical expertise and configuration.

Steps:

Create an ECS Cluster: Define the cluster configuration, including the number of instances and instance type.

Create a Task Definition: Define the Docker image for your Elixir application and any necessary environment variables.

Create a Service: Deploy your task definition as a service and configure load balancing and scaling.

Key Considerations:

Security: Implement strong security measures, such as using strong passwords, enabling MFA, and configuring security groups and IAM roles appropriately.

Monitoring: Use tools like CloudWatch to monitor your application's performance and health.

Scaling: Configure auto-scaling to automatically adjust the number of instances based on load.

Backup and Recovery: Implement regular backups and disaster recovery plans.

Cost Optimization: Use AWS Cost Explorer to analyze your costs and optimize your resource usage.

By carefully considering these factors and choosing the right deployment strategy, you can deploy reliable and scalable Elixir applications on AWS.

Chapter 10

Advanced Elixir Topics

10.1 OTP Behaviors

OTP (Open Telecom Platform) is a framework for building fault-tolerant, distributed systems in Erlang. Elixir inherits this powerful framework, enabling developers to create robust and scalable applications. OTP behaviors are a set of design patterns that provide a structured approach to building concurrent and distributed systems.

Common OTP Behaviors:

GenServer:

A general-purpose server process that can handle requests, maintain state, and respond to queries.

Ideal for building stateful services, such as databases, caches, and message queues.

Supervisor:

Manages a group of child processes.

Monitors child processes for failures and restarts them as needed.

Provides a hierarchical structure for organizing processes.

Worker:

A simple process that performs tasks and exits when finished.

Often used for background tasks, such as file I/O or network operations.

Agent:

A simple process that stores and updates state.

Useful for managing global state or configuration data.

Supervisor:

Manages a group of child processes.

Monitors child processes for failures and restarts them as needed.

Provides a hierarchical structure for organizing processes.

Key Benefits of Using OTP Behaviors:

Fault Tolerance: OTP behaviors provide mechanisms for handling errors and failures, ensuring system reliability.

Scalability: OTP applications can be easily scaled horizontally by adding more nodes to the cluster.

Concurrency: OTP supports efficient handling of concurrent processes, allowing for high throughput and responsiveness.

Modularity: OTP behaviors promote modularity and code reusability.

By understanding and effectively using OTP behaviors, you can build robust, scalable, and maintainable Elixir applications.

10.2 Process Registry and Discovery in Elixir

Elixir, built on the Erlang VM, provides powerful mechanisms for managing and discovering processes. This enables the creation of complex, distributed systems.

Process Registry

The Process Registry is a global registry that allows processes to store and retrieve other processes. It's a key tool for discovering and communicating with processes.

Key Operations:

Registering a Process:

Elixir

```elixir
Process.register(self(), :my_process_name)
```

Looking Up a Process:

Elixir

```elixir
pid = Process.whereis(:my_process_name)
```

Sending a Message to a Registered Process:

Elixir

```elixir
send(pid, {:message, data})
```

Process Discovery

In larger distributed systems, discovering processes can be more complex. Elixir provides various mechanisms for process discovery:

1. Dynamic Supervisor:

A supervisor that starts and stops child processes dynamically based on certain conditions.

Can be used to create and manage a pool of worker processes.

2. ETS Tables:

Distributed hash tables that can be used to store process information.

Can be used to implement a global registry for processes.

3. Distributed Erlang:

Allows processes to communicate across multiple nodes in a cluster.

Enables distributed process discovery and coordination.

Key Considerations:

Process Naming: Use meaningful names for processes to improve readability.

Error Handling: Implement proper error handling mechanisms to prevent process failures from cascading.

Monitoring: Use tools like `iex` and `Observer` to monitor the health and performance of your processes.

Security: Consider security implications when using distributed processes, especially in production environments.

By effectively using process registry and discovery mechanisms, you can build complex, distributed Elixir applications that are scalable, fault-tolerant, and reliable.

10.3 Error Handling and Supervision in Elixir

Elixir, built on the Erlang VM, provides robust mechanisms for handling errors and ensuring system reliability.

Error Handling

In Elixir, errors are typically represented as `{:error, reason}` tuples. You can handle errors using pattern matching in `receive` blocks or `try/catch` expressions.

Example:

Elixir
```
try do
  # Code that might raise an error
  1 / 0
rescue
  e -> IO.puts "Error: #{inspect e}"
end
```

Supervision

Supervision is a core concept in OTP. A supervisor process monitors its child processes and restarts them if they fail. This ensures system reliability and fault tolerance.

Types of Supervisors:

One-for-one: Restarts each failed child process individually.

One-for-all: Restarts all child processes when one fails.

Simple One-for-One: Restarts a failed child process once and then terminates the supervisor.

Example:

```elixir
Elixir
defmodule MySupervisor do
  use Supervisor

  def start_link do
    Supervisor.start_link(__MODULE__, :start_link, [])
  end

  def init(_) do
    children = [
      worker(MyWorker, [arg1, arg2])
    ]
    Supervisor.init(children, strategy: :one_for_one)
  end
end
```

Key Considerations for Error Handling and Supervision:

Logging: Use Logger to log errors and exceptions for debugging and monitoring.

Retry Mechanisms: Implement retry strategies for transient errors.

Circuit Breakers: Use circuit breakers to prevent cascading failures.

Monitoring: Monitor your system's health using tools like `Observer` or third-party monitoring solutions.

Testing: Write comprehensive tests to ensure your error handling and supervision strategies are effective.

By effectively using error handling and supervision, you can build robust and reliable Elixir applications that can recover from failures and continue to operate smoothly.

www.ingramcontent.com/pod-product-compliance
Lightning Source LLC
LaVergne TN
LVHW051740050326
832903LV00023B/1028